Written by Nikki Fotheringham

Photography by Ian Fotheringham

Designed and Published by Jib Strategic

ISBN: 978-0-9939954-2-2
First Edition

For Jill, who hates to cook.

———

My mum, bless her, hates cooking. When I was old
enough to reach the counter top, she taught
me how to make spaghetti in the hopes that I would
save the family from the inevitability that was scurvy.
So I learned to cook from a Julia Childs cookbook I
found propping up the broken end of the bookcase.
While Julia may not have been a great reference for
cooking on an open fire, she certainly fanned the
flames of my culinary passions.

Whether you are camping, hiking, climbing, paddling,
biking or lazing in your backyard, you should be eating
wonderful meals with friends around that fundamental
symbol of warmth and comfort; the campfire.

And if I am able to share a recipe with you that makes
that moment more enjoyable, that makes a meal
memorable, then I will consider this a life well lived.

Time for Adventure!

Introduction

Instant noodles are for chumps! When you're out on an adventure, being your bad-ass self, you deserve only the best campfire cuisine.

Eat like a king when you're playing in the dirt with these easy recipes that are optimized for those living out of a backpack. Of course, they also work for car camping, backyard barbecues and even in your own kitchen, so let's dig in!

Table of Contents

Get Packing!   8

Wakey Wakey, Eggs & Bakey   12

I've Got a Hunch, it's Time for Lunch!   30

Winner, Winner Campfire Dinner   72

Just Desserts   118

On the Side   130

Scary Stuff   142

Packing, Cooling & Storing Food

Freeze your food before you leave, especially meat (marinate this before freezing) and cheese products. You can keep things frozen longer by packing them in foil cold bags or wrapping them in newspaper. Use the newspaper to start your fires when you get to your campsite. You can further insulate your frozen foods by wrapping them in clothing.

Planning on staying on one campsite? Take small coolers if you can. Pack one for each two-day food cycle so that you aren't opening the cooler all the time. If you are packing in your food, pack a flattened cardboard box. At your campsite, reconstruct the box, then place your newspaper-wrapped frozen items in it. You can further insulate with clothing. Place in a shady spot.

Always (always!) hang your food. Losing a couple of meals (and possibly other bits) to wild animals will ruin your trip in two shakes of a raccoon's tail. Never keep food in your tent. Hang food by throwing a rope over a branch that is at least 200 feet (60 meters) from your campsite. Tie the rope to your pack and hoist it at least 12-15 feet (3.5 to 4.5 meters) into the air. Tie off the rope with one of these handy knots:

How to Tie a Clove Hitch:

Packing well will mean you don't spend hours rummaging through bags and coolers every time you need something. If possible, pack cooking utensils and ingredients you will use every day in one pack. In another, pack the ingredients for each meal together in a sealable plastic bag in the order that you will use them. I pack meals and then the clothing I will need for that day to insulate my cold foods. For example: I pack the dinner for the last day on the bottom, followed by lunch and then breakfast on the top. Then I pack my clothing on top of that. Next, food for day two... and so on. It's genius really. Get rid of unnecessary packaging and repack foods into sealable plastic bags so that they take up less space.

Don't wash dishes in bodies of water, especially if you are using soap. Bury the suds at least 200 feet (60 meters) from the water. Ensure that you always use camping detergent that won't damage the environment.

Use sand to remove stubborn food from the bottom of pots and bury the sand (with your suds) far away from your campsite.

How to Tie a Reef Knot:

How to Make a Campfire

It sounds easy enough right? Match, wood... no brainer. But after thirty minutes on your knees huffing and puffing only to have your paltry fire smolder out, you know the struggle. Every seasoned fire starter will swear by their particular method, but there are some basic tenants that are true for all fires.

- Never use green or wet wood. That means you never tear bark or branches off living trees. Find deadfall to use or pack in your firewood.
- Birch bark makes the best natural fire starter. It's practically invincible.
- Never use fuel on a cooking fire. You're better than that.
- If the wood is very dry, you can pack up the whole fire and then toss in a match and walk away. Don't look back; badasses never do. Actually, look back... fires are dangerous!
- If the wood is not well seasoned or it has been raining, start really small. Just a little birch bark and a few small twigs, then slowly build it up. Pack the rest of the wood close to the fire so it can dry.
- Oxygen; you need it, fires need it. Always pack your kindling with gaps so the air can get in. If your fire is struggling, blow gently on kindling.
- Fire starters can be made from candle wax and dryer lint; just put the lint in the bottom of an egg carton and pour melted wax over it. Break off each egg section and use to light your fire.
- In a pinch, crayons and corn chips (like Dorritos) work really well too.

Building a Snack Fire

This is a good one for boiling water or cooking smores and will work nicely for heat too. It's quick and easy. Place a couple of balled up pieces of paper or some birch bark in the center, then lay the kindling around in a teepee style. If the wood is wet, start small. Leave gaps between the kindling so air can get in. Light the paper or bark and blow gently on the flames.

Building a Cooking Fire

Place the bark or paper in the center with a little kindling on it. Now build a square around the kindling in a 'log cabin' formation, alternating parallel logs which leave gaps for air to get in.

You can make a ring of stones around the main fire & then a channel with parallel rows of stones coming off one side of your stone fire circle. This is your cooking area. Use a stick to scrape your coals over to the cooking channel. This means you can continue to generate hot coals in your fire & move them over to the cooking area when you need them. This helps you to regulate the temperature and you won't get caught with a dying fire and an uncooked breakfast.

Wakey Wakey

eggs & bakey

Get Up! Breakfast's On!

Hey there sleepy head. We know you need to prepare for your day of hiking, climbing, rowing, playing, swimming and snoozing, so here are some hearty morning meals to fuel your fun.

Tips to Start Your Day

 Check yourself for ticks regularly. If you find one, don't pull it off as the head may get stuck beneath the surface of your skin. Instead, soak a cotton ball in soap and hold against the tick for a minute. It will easily come away when you remove the cotton ball. If the tick has been there for a while, keep it and have it tested for Lyme disease.

 Itchy bites or rashes from poison ivy? Make a paste out of baking soda and water and rub it on the affected area for instant relief. In a pinch, toothpaste with baking soda will work too.

What's on the Menu?

Breakfast Burrito with Chorizo 14
Fancy-Ass French Toast 16
Good Old Fry Up 18
Homemade Pancake Mix 20
Lumberjack Special 22
Toad in a Hole 24
No-Bake Morning Glory Bars 26
Fried Green Tomatoes 28

Breakfast
Burrito
with Chorizo

What You Need

- 4 Eggs
- 4 tbsp. Oil
- 1 Avocado (sliced)
- 1 Onion (sliced)

- 1 Chorizo sausage (thinly sliced)
- Salt and pepper to taste
- 4 Burritos

Instructions

Break eggs into a bowl and whisk. Set aside. Heat 2 tablespoons of oil in a pan and gently fry the onions until translucent. Add the chorizo, salt and pepper to taste. Fry for 2 minutes. Spoon chorizo mixture onto the burritos. Put the pan back on the coals and add the two remaining tablespoons of oil and scramble the eggs. Pop the eggs on the burritos and top with the sliced avocado and BAM! you've got yourself a badass breakfast burrito.

Serves 4

 # Tips

If you are making this dish in the first couple of days of your trip, add cheese and salsa.

If you are making this dish on the last few days of your trip, pack an avocado that isn't ripe so it can ripen while you travel or substitute this for a can of salsa.

For a vegetarian option, omit the chorizo and add fried tofu to the avocado and onion.

Want a little spice in your life? Add chili flakes or hot sauce.

Fancy-Ass French Toast

What You Need

- Baguette
- 2 Bananas
- 3 Eggs
- 2 tbsp. Water

- Salt
- 4 tbsp. Oil
- Maple syrup

Instructions

Thickly slice your Baguette. Make a small incision in each slice to create a delicious little bread envelope. Slice the bananas and insert into your bread envelope.

In a bowl, mix the eggs and a pinch of salt with 2 tablespoons of water. Place your pan on the fire or camp stove and warm to a medium heat. Dip your bread and banana slices in the egg mixture and fry gently until brown on both sides. Place on a plate, drizzle with maple syrup and serve hot.

Serves 4

Tips

The bread doesn't have to be fresh so this makes a great breakfast for the second day of your trip.

Got a lot to do today? Ramp up your energy by adding chocolate chips to your fancy-ass French toast (yup, that just happened!)

Forego the maple syrup and swap the bananas with strawberry jam and cream cheese for a New York Cheesecake version that will make you the king (or queen) of camping breakfast.

Use sliced bread and make banana sandwiches which you can dip in the egg mixture before frying.

Good Old Fry Up

What You Need

- 1/4 Cup oil
- 1/4 Loaf bread (cubed)
- 3 Eggs (beaten)
- 2 tbsp. Water

- Salt and pepper to taste
- 1 Cup chopped ham or bacon

Instructions

Heat the oil in a large pan over the coals. Add the ham or bacon. Add bread and fry until golden brown. Add the eggs, water, salt & pepper to taste. Cook until eggs are done, stirring occasionally.

Serves 4-6

 ## Tips

Add cheese on top if you are making this in the first couple of days of your trip.

Substitute chorizo or salami for the ham or bacon if you are making this later on in your trip.

For a vegetarian option, omit the ham or bacon and add onions and tomatoes.

Homemade Pancakes

What You Need

- 4 1/2 Cups flour
- 2 tbsp. Baking powder
- 1 tsp. Salt
- 1 1/2 Cups shortening

- 1 1/2 Cups non-fat powdered milk
- 1/2 Egg
- 1/2 Cup water
- Oil

Instructions

Mix the flour, baking powder, salt, and milk powder together. Rub in shortening so it resembles bread crumbs. Store in a sealable plastic bag or a Mason jar. Store this little puppy in your backpack until you are ready for pancake heaven. Then add the egg and enough water to make a pancake batter. Fry in a pan with a little oil over warm coals. Serve with fruit, maple syrup, peanut butter or butter.

Serves 4-6

 # Tips

Substitute powdered egg if you are planning a really long trip.

Shortening does not need to be refrigerated, so this mix can last up to 6 months.

If you store the dry ingredients in a sealable plastic bag, add the liquids straight into the bag, mush it around until your pancake mixture is ready, then cut a corner off the bottom of the bag and pipe the mixture into your pan. This is the perfect opportunity to get creative with those pancake shapes and unleash your inner artist!

Lumberjack Special

What You Need

- 12 Sausages
- 4 Eggs
- 2 Tomatoes (diced)
- 4 Green onions (diced)
- Salt and pepper to taste
- Foil

Instructions

Lay three of the sausages on a large piece of foil. Fold up the edges a little then break an egg over the sausages and top with the diced tomato and green onion. Season with salt and pepper. Fold the corners of the foil up so it tents over the egg. Cook 15-20 minutes over medium coals or until sausages are cooked through.

Serves 4

 # Tips

Substitute chorizo or salami for the sausages if you aren't making this on the first couple of days of your trip.

Use soya sausages for a vegetarian option

You can add cheese, bacon or cooked potatoes to supersize this breakfast.

Toad in a Hole

What You Need

- 4 Rashers of bacon
- 4 Slices of bread
- 4 Eggs
- Extra oil

Instructions

Fry up the bacon until crispy and set aside. Leave the bacon fat in the skillet. Use a camping cup to cut a hole in the middle of each slice of bread. Lay the bread in the skillet and brown on one side. Turn the slice over, now crack an egg into the hole. Fry until the egg is done and slide bread onto a plate. The bacon fat may not see you through all four slices so use the extra oil if the bread starts to stick. Crumble the bacon over the top.

Serves 4

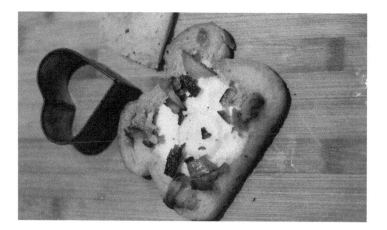

 ## Tips

Note: No toads were harmed in the making of this dish.

If you are making this after the second day, use salami or chorizo instead of bacon.

For a vegetarian option, top with chopped tomato.

No-Bake Morning Glory Bars

What You Need

- 1 Cup instant oats
- 1/2 Cup peanut butter
- 1/4 Cup honey
- 1 tbsp. Melted coconut oil
- 3 tbsp. Chocolate chips (optional)
- Pinch of salt
- 1/4 tsp. Ground cinnamon
- 1/4 Cup of one of these: raisins, nuts, dried fruits, coconut

Instructions

Rise and shine with these delicious little amazeballs! Simply mix the ingredients together and roll into little balls. Store in a sealable plastic bag. Ready to eat.

Serves 4

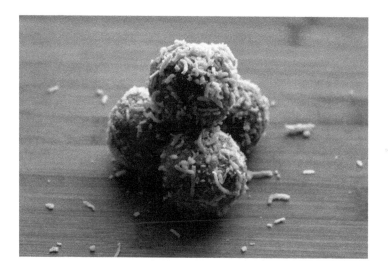

 # Tips

Use maple syrup instead of honey. These can be made with trail mix too.

Make a few extra balls and take them along to snack on while you're on the trail.

Make these before you leave and keep them in the fridge for a couple of days but be warned, they are so good you may just eat them before you set foot out the door.

Fried Green Tomatoes

What You Need

- 4 Green tomatoes (sliced)
- 1 Cup of flour
- 1 Beaten Egg
- Salt and pepper to taste
- 4 tbsp. Oil

Instructions

Green tomatoes are firmer and won't get squished in your bag.
Still, pack with care as they are delicate.

Dip tomato slices in the flour, then in the egg, and then back in
the flour. Fry on both sides until lightly browned. Season with
salt and pepper.

Serves 4

 # Tips

Use 1/2 cup flour and 1/2 cup cornmeal for a more authentic
Southern flavor.

HP sauce and fried green tomatoes; a match made in heaven.

I've got a ~~Hunch~~ It's Time for Lunch!

Fuel Your Fun!

Whether you are taking a brief reprieve from an active day or simply rolling out of the hammock for a bite to eat, don't let it be a handful of trail mix or a can of salty soup. You're better than that! These easy recipes are delightfully delicious and will have you munching on your luncheon in no time at all.

Tips to Start Your Day

Freeze water in water bottles to keep food cool over the first couple of days and for drinking towards the end of your trip.

Use a large sealable plastic bag or (if you're like me) blow some air into the bag of wine you brought and use as a comfy pillow. Wine bags double as a handy flotation device.

What's on the Menu?

Beet and Feta Salad	32
Toasted Chicken Sandwich	34
Juan in a Million Tacos	36
Couscous Salad	38
Zucchini Couscous	40
Toastie Wraps	42
Mozzarella Tomato Towers	44
Pita Pan Toasties	46
Popcorn Pockets	48
Onion and Cheese Bread	50
Tomato Peach Salad	52
Roasted Potato Salad	54
Potato Skins	56
Pull-Apart Pizza Bread	58
Nature's Nachos	60
Grilled Steak Sandwich	62
Toasted Ham and Cheese Sandwich	64
Easy Peasy Pizza	66
Baked Avocado	68
Carrot Salad	70

Beet and Feta Salad

What You Need

- 4 Beets
- Pinch of salt
- 2 tbsp. White vinegar
- 1/4 Red onion finely chopped
- Feta cheese

Instructions

Warning; once you enjoy beets this way, there's no going back. Ready? Then lettuce turnip the beets!

Pop the beets into a pot of boiling water, or place them in foil on the coals. Poke a fork in them to see when they are done. Leave to cool. Peel off the skin and cut into thin slices. Mix in a bowl with onion, salt, vinegar and crumbled feta.

Serves 4

 # Tips

Make this recipe before you go. Buy a bag of beets and either roast them in the oven (for sweet beets) or boil them on the stove. Slice them up and pop them into Mason jars with a mixture of 1/4 vinegar to 3/4 water and a little salt. This makes several jars and means that you can make beet salad at will. Transfer beets to plastic bags or containers before going camping.

Toasted Chicken Sandwich

What You Need

- 4 Chicken breasts (barbecued)
- 6 tbsp. Mayonnaise
- Salt to taste
- 8 Slices of bread

Instructions

This is a really great lunch to make the day after a chicken barbecue. Break the chicken up into small chunks and mix with mayonnaise and salt. Divide into four and spread over 4 slices of bread. Place a second slice of bread on top to finish off the sandwiches. Grill on both sides until golden brown. This is seriously delicious!

Serves 4

 # Tips

If you are making this meal in the first couple of days, spread butter over the bread for a richer taste.

You can lightly oil the grill to prevent the bread from sticking.

If you are making this meal after the first couple of days, freeze the uncooked chicken and pack it in a small cooler or wrap it in newspaper to keep fresh.

Juan in a Million Tacos

What You Need

- 2 tbsp. Oil
- 1 lb. Ground beef (450g)
- Taco spice (see page 132)
- 2 Tomatoes (chopped)
- 1 Small onion (chopped)

- Cheese
- 1 Avocado (sliced)
- Tortillas
- Foil

Instructions

Heat the oil in a skillet over a medium heat. Brown the beef, add taco spice and cook for two minutes. Build your tacos by adding beef, tomatoes, onion, cheese and avocado to the tortillas. Wrap tacos in foil and place them on the grill for 2 minutes

Serves 4

 # Tips

Use dehydrated soya mince for a vegetarian option or if you are cooking this meal after the first two days of your trip. Omit the cheese as well and be sure to pack an unripe avocado and tomatoes which can ripen over the first couple of days.

Use a bag of store-bought taco spice if you don't want to make your own.

Couscous Salad

What You Need

- 1 Cup water
- 1 Cup of couscous
- 1 Small red onion
  (finely diced)

- 1/2 Cup raisins
- Handful of almonds
  (chopped)
- Salt and pepper to taste

Instructions

Bring the water to a boil and add couscous. Remove pot from the heat. Cover and let it stand for about 5 minutes. Fluff couscous with a fork and allow to cool. Add the rest of the ingredients and enjoy!

Serves 4

 # Tips

Optional extras include mayonnaise or balsamic vinegar, dried apricots (diced), chickpeas, mint or parsley.

Zucchini Couscous

What You Need

- 3 Large zucchinis
- 1 tbsp. Oil
- 1 Cup water
- Vegetable stock cube
- 2/3 Cup of couscous

Instructions

Slice zucchini and fry in the oil until cooked but firm (about 4 minutes). Add water and stock cube and bring to a boil. Add couscous and remove your pot from the heat. Cover and let it stand for about 5 minutes. Fluff couscous with a fork, then cover and let it stand for another 5 minutes.

Serves 4

 # Tips

This makes a great side dish for stew or chili or bulk it up by adding other veggies like canned tomatoes, beans, carrots and onions.

Add chorizo or salami for a protein boost.

Toastie Wraps

What You Need

- 8 Tortillas
- 2 Cups grated cheese
- 2 Tomatoes (thinly sliced)
- 1 Small onion (thinly sliced)
- Salt and pepper

Instructions

Lay four tortillas on the hand grill. Top with grated cheese, sliced tomatoes and onion and season with salt and pepper. Place the second tortilla on top of each wrap and close grill. Grill on both sides until golden brown.

Serves 4

 # Tips

You can add bacon, chorizo, salami or leftover barbecue meat for a meat lover's option.

You can lightly oil the grill to prevent sticking.

Don't have a grill? Wrap these puppies in foil and place directly on medium coals until the cheese melts and the tortillas brown.

Mozzarella Tomato Towers

What You Need

- 1 lb. (450g) Mozzarella cheese
- 4 Large Italian tomatoes
- 1 Large bunch of basil
- 2 tbsp. Olive oil

Instructions

Cut thick slices of tomatoes and mozzarella. Start with a slice of tomato, then add a slice of cheese and top with basil leaves. You should be able to get a few layers out of each tomato and 100g (3.5 oz.) cheese to make 4 towers of cheesy goodness. Drizzle with olive oil and serve.

Serves 4

 # Tips

Pop these cheesy towers on a square of foil and tent the foil over the top. Now place them on the grill to get a melted cheese delight.

Put the tower in a burger bun and roast over the flames for a great vegetarian burger option.

Lashings of balsamic vinegar will add a little zing and feel free to experiment with different cheeses.

Pita Pan Toasties

What You Need

- 1lb. (450g) Boneless chicken breast cut into strips
- 2 tbsp. Corn flour
- 1 tsp. Ground cumin
- 1 tsp. Paprika
- 1/4 tsp. Chili powder
- Plastic bag

- 2 tbsp. Oil
- 1 Red bell pepper
- 1/2 Red onion (finely chopped)
- 1 Tomato (finely chopped)
- 1 Cup grated cheese
- 4 Pita breads

Instructions

Mix the corn flour, cumin, paprika and chili powder in the plastic bag. Toss in the chicken strips and shake that bag ... shake it real good! Actually, just shake it until the chicken is coated. In a frying pan, heat the oil and fry chicken strips until browned. While your chicken is cooking, place the red pepper directly on the coals. Turn gently and allow the skin to blister and blacken all the way around. Now throw that sucker into the plastic bag you used for the chicken (of course, you've removed any left over cornflour mixture). Close the plastic bag and let the pepper sweat. Remove the pepper, peel off the blackened skin and slice.

Cut your pita pockets in half and place one half on your handheld grill. Spread the onion and tomato, chicken and bell pepper on the pita that is on the grill and top with cheese. Place the top of the pita back on and close the grill. Grill on both sides until the pita turns golden brown.

Serves 4

 # Tips

Mix the corn flour, cumin, paprika and chili pepper in a plastic bag before you leave so that it's easier to transport.

If you are using a thin plastic bag, ensure that the pepper isn't hot enough to burn right through it.

You can use chicken from a barbecue you had the night before. Use the cumin, paprika and chili to season and forgo the corn flour.

Is roasting the bell pepper too much trouble? No problem; just slice the raw pepper and use it instead. Of course it's not going to taste as awesome... just saying.

Popcorn Pockets

What You Need

- 2 tbsp. Popcorn kernels
- 2 tbsp. Oil
- Salt

- Foil
- String
- Stick

Instructions

In an 18-inch (45cm) square of foil, place the popcorn and the oil. Pull up the edges and squish them together at the top to make a little foil packet, leaving plenty of room for popped corn. Tie the foil top with string and tie the other end of the string to the stick. Use the stick like a fishing rod to dangle your popcorn pocket over the fire until the corn is popped. Open your pocket & season with salt.

Serves 1

 ## Tips

If you're making popcorn at the start of your trip, you better be smothering it in melted butter!

You need to bob the pocket up and down to keep the kernels moving so they don't burn or stick.

Season your popcorn with vinegar, hot sauce or lemon juice.

Onion and Cheese Bread

What You Need

- 1 Baguette
- 2 tbsp. Butter
- 1 Cup grated cheddar cheese
- 2 tbsp. Mustard

- Salt to taste
- 1 Medium onion thinly sliced
- Foil

Instructions

Slice bread in half lengthwise. Spread butter on the top half and mustard on the bottom half. Spread the onions over the mustard. Spread the cheese over the onion slices. Put the two halves together, coat the top of the bread with olive oil and wrap it in the foil. Place on the grill for 20 minutes, turning regularly.

Serves 4

 # Tips

Add crushed garlic for a garlic onion bread, chilies for a zing or mango chutney for something a little sweeter.

Feel free to use dijon or flavored mustards; I know you're fancy like that.

For day 2-4, you can use olive oil instead of butter or freeze the butter and cheese before you leave & keep them wrapped in newspaper. Keep your pack in a shady, cool spot.

Meat lovers can add chorizo, salami, cooked bacon or ham.

Tomato Peach Salad

What You Need

- 4 Large tomatoes (diced)
- 4 Peaches (cut in wedges)
- 1 Red onion (finely sliced)
- 2 tbsp. Apple cider vinegar
- Salt and pepper to taste

Instructions

Place tomatoes, peaches and onion into a bowl and drizzle with vinegar and season to taste. Mix and serve.

Serves 4-6

 ## Tips

Use canned peaches if you aren't making this salad on the first day of your trip. Take green tomatoes and pack them carefully so that they don't get squashed. They will ripen on the trip.

Want to blow your mind? Of course you do! Place the peach slices on the grill for two minutes on each side. The peaches will be sweeter and tastier.

Leave the skins on too - you can never have too much fiber!

Roasted Potato Salad

What You Need

- 6 Fire-roasted potatoes
  (see tips if you are all out
  of these)

- 3 Green onions (sliced)

- 1/2 Cup mayonnaise

- 1 tsp. Apple cider vinegar

- Pinch of salt

Instructions

You can wrap potatoes in foil and roast them on the coals the day before for this recipe. Dice potatoes and place in a large bowl. Add 2 of the onions, mayonnaise, vinegar and salt and mix well. Garnish with the last onion because you're classy that way.

Serves 4

 ## Tips

Don't have roasted potatoes? Cut your potatoes in quarters, brush with olive oil and place straight on the grill. Turn often until cooked.

Raining? Dice the potatoes and boil in a pot of water until cooked, but firm.

I leave my potato skins on — there's a ton of nutritional value in them and they taste good too. Feel free to peel yours if you prefer.

You can fry up the skins for some potato skin goodness, see our recipe on the next page!

Potato Skins

What You Need

- The peels from 6 scrubbed
  potatoes (use potatoes for
  potato salad on page 55 or
  shepherd's pie on page 110)
- 2 tbsp. Oil
- Pinch of salt

**For the dipping sauce
(optional)**

- Avocado
- 2 tbsp. Mayonnaise
- Salt and pepper to taste
- 1 tsp. Apple cider vinegar
- Hot sauce (optional)

Instructions

I really do love woodland creatures, but I just can't seem to get them to do my housework. After your fellow campers taste this little woodland treat, they will be clambering to wash the dishes if you promise to give them just a little more...

Gently heat the oil and add the potato peels. Sauté gently for 5-10 minutes until golden brown. Sprinkle with salt.

For the dipping sauce; mash the avocado, mayonnaise, salt, pepper, vinegar and hot sauce (optional) together to form a delicious, finger-licking dip for your hot potatoes.

Serves 4

Pull-Apart Pizza Bread

What You Need

- 12 oz (340 grams) Mozzarella cheese (thinly sliced)
- 12 oz (340 grams) Pepperoni (sliced)

- 1 Green onion (finely sliced)
- Foil
- Bread

Instructions

Slice the bread horizontally and vertically so you make a checkered pattern, but don't slice all the way through. Between your little bread squares, slip in slices of pepperoni and cheese and sprinkle the onion in there as well. Wrap in foil and place on the grill for about 15 minutes or until your cheese has melted. Now pull the squares apart and enjoy the cheesiness!

Serves 4

 # Tips

Chorizo makes a nice substitute for the pepperoni.

Feel free to use other kinds of cheese like brie and cheddar.

You can add a salsa dipping sauce if you have room in your pack.

Nature's Nachos

What You Need

- 4 Tortillas
- Can of salsa

- Grated Cheese

Instructions

Place the tortillas on a grill over medium coals. Turn them regularly until they are brown and crispy. Break the tortillas into pieces and place in a skillet or on a sheet of foil. Layer the salsa over the top and sprinkle the cheese over the salsa. If you are cooking in the skillet, using the lid will help the cheese to melt. If you are using foil, tent the foil over the top. You can add extra toppings like refried beans, peppers, guacamole or sour cream. This is better than a pit full of pandas!

Serves 4

 # Tips

If you are making nachos after the first two days, take a block of frozen cheese so it lasts longer. Use a knife to cut the cheese (insert appropriate joke about cutting the cheese) into very thin slices.

Grilled Steak Sandwich

What You Need

- 2 Large steaks
- 1 Red pepper
- 1 Medium onion
  (thinly sliced)

- 1 Plastic bag
- Salt and Pepper to taste
- Cheese (optional)
- 4 Fresh bread rolls

Instructions

My biggest disappointment with sandwiches is that they contain neither sand nor (more importantly) witches. But still, you can rekindle the love with these delicious steak sandwiches.

Barbecue your steak over the fire, seasoned to taste. Place the red pepper right on the coals, turning regularly, until the outside blisters and turns black. Pop the pepper into the plastic bag and seal. Leave the pepper to sweat.

Slice the steak into thin pieces and arrange on the rolls. Top with sliced onion and season to taste. Open the plastic bag and remove the pepper. The charred skin should easily rub off leaving a sweet, juicy pepper inside. Discard the seeds and slice finely. Add to the sandwiches & top with cheese.

Serves 4

 # Tips

Omit cheese if you are serving this after the first few days. Freeze the steaks if you want them to last longer.

Frying the onions will definitely add to the flavor of this meal. You can also wrap the rolls in foil and pop them back on the coals for a minute or two to melt the cheese for a cheddar melt steak.

Toasted Ham and Cheese Sandwich

What You Need

- 4 Slices of Ham
- 4 tbsp. Mayonnaise
- Cheese

- Salt to taste
- 8 Slices of bread

Instructions

So you think you know ham and cheese? Well wait until you taste this one... Mind. Blown!

Lay four slices of bread on the grill. Place one piece of ham on each slice of bread and top with cheese. Spread one tablespoon of mayonnaise on each of the remaining slices of bread and place them on top of the cheese to make four sandwiches. Grill on both sides until golden brown.

Serves 4

 Tips

Spread butter over the bread for a richer taste if you are making this on the first day or two.

You can lightly oil the grill to prevent the bread from sticking.

For a vegetarian option, use tomato instead of ham.

Easy Peasy Pizza

What You Need

- 1 1/2 Cups self-rising flour

- 1/2 tsp. Salt

- 1/3 Cup warm water

- 3 tbsp. Olive oil

- 1 Can tomato paste

- 1 Medium onion (diced)

- 1 Cup cheese (grated)

Instructions

Mix the flour, salt, warm water and olive oil into a firm pizza dough.
Oil a skillet and press the dough into the bottom of the pan. Smear
tomato paste on top and sprinkle onion over the top. Top your pizza
with cheese and place over medium hot coals. Place a lid on the
skillet and bake until the crust has browned around the edges.
I cook these right on the grill and put the skillet over the top to
keep the heat in so the cheese gets nice and brown.

Serves 4

 # Tips

Substitute the tomato paste for fresh slices of tomato if weight is
an issue or with a can of tomato sauce if you prefer.

Add bacon, avocado, ham, pepperoni, sausages or any other pizza
topping of choice.

Freeze cheese if you are making this after the first day of your trip.

Baked Avocado

What You Need

- 2 Avocados
- Salt
- Pepper
- Chili flakes
- 1 Medium tomato
  (finely chopped)

- 1 Medium onion
  (finely chopped)
- Feta cheese (optional)
- Foil

Instructions

Cut the avocado in half and remove the pit. Use a spoon to scrape a little of the avocado out to make a bigger space to hold the filling. Mix the avocado you just removed in a separate bowl with the salt, pepper, chili, tomato and onion. Spoon into the avocado and top with feta cheese. Wrap in foil (shiny side in) and place over hot coals for 15-20 minutes until the avocado begins to brown.

Serves 4

 # Tips

If you are making this meal after the first two days of your trip, omit the cheese.

Tent the foil over the top of the avocado if you are using cheese to prevent it from sticking.

Carrot Salad

What You Need

- 4 Large carrots (grated)
- 1/2 Cup raisins (optional)
- 1 Can pineapple pieces

Instructions

Grate the carrots into a medium bowl, add the pineapple pieces and about 4 tablespoons of the juice and the raisins. Mix and serve.

Serves 4-6

 ## Tips

If you are eating this salad in the first two days, you can make it before you leave home.

You can use a fresh pineapple too.

Don't have a small grater? Julienne the carrots (cut into thin slices).

Add hemp hearts and pumpkin seeds (pepitas) for added protein and flavor.

Winner, Winner Campfire Dinner

What you've been waiting for...

You've worked hard, you've played hard and now it's time to enjoy the fruits of your labor! Dinner's on us with these easy, fun and delicious recipes that will make you the most popular camper in this neck of the woods.

Best Camping Tips Ever!

 Make your own natural insect repellent for a bug-free summer. Mix 12 drops lemon eucalyptus oil, 12 drops citronella oil, 12 drops orange oil and 1/2 cup witch hazel in a spray bottle and apply liberally.

What's on the Menu?

Campfire Bannock	74
Balsamic Vinegar Asparagus	76
BBQ Pie	78
Bobotie in a Squash	80
Bacon Potatoes	82
Bunny Chow	84
Navajo Fry Bread	86
Corn on the Cob	88
Beer Bread	90
Wheat Heart Campfire Bread	92
Caramelized Onions on the Grill	94
Catch of the Day	96
Chicken Foil Folders	98
Chicken on a Beer Can	100
Potato Pockets	102
Fried Bass with Salt & Vinegar Chips, Mate	104
Good Ol' Stew	106
Atomic Boogaloo Chili	108
Shepherd's Pie in a Pot	110
Veggie Kebabs	112
Sticky Pork Chops	114
Marinated Flank Steak	116

Campfire Bannock

What You Need

- 2 1/2 Cups flour
- 2 tsp. Baking powder
- 1/2 tsp. Sugar

- 1/2 tsp. Salt
- 3 tbsp. Oil
- 1 Cup water

Instructions

Bannock has been a staple among the Aboriginal people of North America for centuries where it was made from moss, lichen, ground plant bulbs, nut meal, corn meal and cattail pollen to name a few traditional ingredients. Consequently, there are as many bannock recipes as the day is long.

Today we are exploring a simple bannock recipe that is really versatile. You can make balls which you flatten with your palm and fry in a pan - use for tacos, burgers, sandwiches etc. Roll balls and pop them on top of a stew to make dumplings. You can also fry in lard, bacon fat or oil and sprinkle with sugar and cinnamon as a treat or follow the traditional method of cooking over the coals on a stick.

————

Mix dry ingredients. Add oil and enough water to form a firm dough that doesn't stick to the hands. Knead for 2 minutes then leave to rest for 30 minutes.

Divide into six portions and flatten with the palm of your hand to form discs. Select a long thin stick and clean off the end with a knife. Form the dough around the stick.

Scrape some of the coals out from the fire on to the edge of your firepit. Hold the stick over the coals, turning frequently until your bannock is brown and cooked through.

Serves 6

Balsamic Vinegar Asparagus

What You Need

- 1 Bunch asparagus spears
- 4 tbsp. Water
- 2 tbsp. Balsamic vinegar
- Salt and pepper to taste

Instructions

In a small pan, bring the water to a boil. Toss in the asparagus and cook until it starts to wilt (about 4 minutes). Add the balsamic vinegar and cook for one more minute. Remove from fire and season with salt and pepper.

Serves 4-6

 ## Tips

If you are cooking this side dish at the beginning of your trip, add butter for a little extra flavor.

BBQ Pie

What You Need

- Leftover BBQ meat (chopped)
- 1 Medium Onion (chopped)
- 2 tbsp. Olive oil
- Salt and pepper
- 3 tbsp. Water

- 1 1/2 Cups flour (plus a little extra for dusting)
- 1/2 Cup vegetable shortening
- 1/2 tsp. Salt
- 1/2 Cup cold water

Instructions

Place olive oil and onion in a pan and fry until translucent. Add the meat, water, salt and pepper and cook for 3 minutes. Leave to cool.

To make your pastry, cut the shortening and flour together until the mixture resembles breadcrumbs. Add the salt and just enough water to form a firm dough.

Knead until combined (don't overwork). Roll out dough on a floured surface (a water bottle will do nicely as a rolling pin) into a long rectangle. Cut the dough in two. Lay the first piece on a handheld grill. Top with your pie filling and then the second piece of dough on top of the filling. Pinch the edges together really well so your filling won't leak out. Close the grill and grill on the fire, turning often, until brown and cooked (about 15 minutes.)

Serves 4

 # Tips

For camping convenience, this recipe has been kept simple, but you can spice up the BBQ meat with paprika, chilies, fresh thyme or rosemary. You can also add a gravy mix to create a more robust filling. If you are making this pie in the first two days, add cheese!

If you don't have leftover BBQ meat, you can BBQ a steak or some chicken for your pie. Pork chops, sausage & venison also work well.

For a vegetarian option, use roasted vegetables, or feta & spinach.

Bake this pie in your metal camping cup instead. Roll out the dough and cut into 8 pieces. Lightly oil each cup and line with dough. Spoon the filling in and top with another piece of dough. Bake on the fire until crust is golden brown.

Bobotie in a Squash

What You Need

- 1 tbsp. Cooking oil
- 350g (0.8 lbs) Ground beef
- 1 Onion, chopped
- 1 Garlic clove, crushed
- 2 tbsp. Garam masala
- 2 tbsp. Chutney
- 1 tbsp. Cider vinegar

- 2 Eggs
- 1 1/2 Cups milk
- 1 Slice white bread
- Large squash with top cut off and seeds hollowed out like you would for a Halloween Jack o' Lantern

Instructions

Heat the oil in a large pan, add ground beef and fry until browned. Add chopped onion, garlic, and garam masala.

Add chutney and apple cider vinegar. Add a little hot water and simmer for 8 – 10 minutes.

Pour 1/2 cup of milk over bread. Mix remaining milk and eggs together. Mash soggy bread into ground beef and cook for one minute. Spoon the beef mixture into the squash. Pour egg mixture over mince. Wrap the squash in foil and place on hot coals. Heap hot coals on top and bake for 40 minutes or until custard browns. Keep adding hot coals from the fire as needed.

Serves 4

 # Tips

If you are making this meal in the first two days of your expedition, use fresh ground beef. For use later in the trip and for a vegetarian option, use dehydrated soya mince.

Add a grated carrot or Granny Smith apple (or both) if you need to bulk it out.

Bacon Potatoes

What You Need

- 4 Medium potatoes (washed)
- 4 Rashers of bacon
- 1 Medium onion (sliced)
- 4 tbsp. Butter or olive oil
- Salt and pepper
- Foil

Instructions

Lay out a sheet of foil and place a potato on the foil. Slice the potato into thin slices 3/4 of the way through, leaving the bottom attached. Cut the rashers of bacon into small pieces and slip these between the potato slices. Dot each potato with 1 tablespoon of butter or pour olive oil over them. Season with salt and pepper. Wrap in the foil and bury in hot coals. Bake for 30-45 minutes or until potatoes are cooked through. Enjoy the bacon potatoey goodness!

Serves 4

 ## Tips

If you are making this meal in the first two days of your expedition, use butter and bacon and add a little cheese on top.

For use later in the trip, use olive oil instead of butter and salami or chorizo instead of bacon.

For a vegetarian option, use tomato instead of meat.

Bunny Chow

What You Need

- 1/2 tsp. Ginger
- 1/4 tsp. Cloves
- 1 tsp. Cinnamon
- 3 Cardamom pods cracked
- 2 tsp. Garam masala
- 1/2 tsp. Cumin
- 1 Garlic clove chopped
- 2 tsp. Turmeric

- 3 tbsp. Oil
- 2 Onions (chopped)
- 2 Tomatoes (chopped)
- 500g Beef, lamb, or chicken
- 2 White potatoes (chopped)
- 1/2 Cup water
- Salt
- Loaf of bread

Instructions

For the Curry: Measure the spices at home and save in a sealable plastic bag or in a plastic container. If you don't want to use these spices, buy a curry spice pouch or bottle of curry sauce instead. You can substitute fresh ginger root if you prefer, just make sure it's finely chopped or grated. This curry isn't hot! For a little heat, add 1 tsp. cayenne pepper or chili powder to taste.

For the Bunny Chow: Heat the oil in a pan and add cloves, garlic, ginger and chopped onions. Fry over a medium heat until onions are translucent. Add cinnamon, cardamom pods, garam masala, cumin, and turmeric and fry for one minute.

Add meat and cook until browned. Now add tomatoes, potatoes, water and salt to taste. Cover and simmer for 30 minutes, stirring occasionally. If your curry sticks, add a little more water.

Remove the lid and let your curry simmer until the sauce is thick and juicy. Cut your loaf into quarters. With the tip of your knife, cut along the inside of the crust about 3/4 of the way through. Gently scoop out the inside of the loaf to make bread 'bowls'. Fill these with the curry and place the inside of the bread on the top. Use the inside of the bread to scoop up the curry and mop up the sauce.

Serves 4

Tips

Use soya mince, beans or vegetables for a vegetarian option.
Use round loaves instead to make bread bowls.

Navajo Fry Bread

What You Need

- 4 Cups flour
- 2 tsp. Baking powder
- 1 tsp. Salt

- 3 tbsp. Oil
- 1 Cup warm water
- Oil for frying

Instructions

Fry bread is a brilliant way to cook bannock that gives you, our intrepid outdoor gourmet, the perfect vehicle for just about anything. Fill them with leftovers or use them to make tacos, breakfast burritos, burgers or hot dogs. Enjoy them as a dessert with a little cinnamon and sugar. Make your life easier by mixing the dry ingredients and keeping them in a sealable bag. Just add the oil and water when you are ready to get your feast on.

Mix dry ingredients. Add oil and enough water to form a firm dough that doesn't stick to the hands. Leave to rest for 30 minutes. Divide into six portions and flatten with the palm of your hand to form discs. Poke a hole in the center to allow the oil to bubble through. Heat the oil in a frying pan over a medium fire. Drop the fry bread in and cook for 2 minutes or until the edges turn brown. Turn over and fry for another two minutes. Are you ready for delicious fry bread goodness?

Serves 6

Corn on the Cob

What You Need

- 4 Sweetcorn on the cob
- Butter

- Salt to taste

Instructions

Soak the corn with the husk on for 30 minutes. Place the corn directly on medium coals. Turn often. The husk will slowly start to burn off. When you start to see the kernels through the husk, remove from the coals, dot with butter and season with salt.

Serves 4

 # Tips

If you are making corn on the cob after the first couple of days, you can omit the butter and season with hot sauce, olive oil, parmesan cheese or garlic salt.

If the husk has been removed from your corn, wrap in foil or cook on the grill instead of on the coals.

Be sure to soak before cooking.

Beer Bread

What You Need

- 3 Cups flour
- 1 tsp. Baking powder
- 3 tbsp. Sugar
- 1 Can beer (warm)

Instructions

Mix dry ingredients and slowly add the beer until you have a soft dough. Knead well and then place in a greased pot or Dutch oven. Cook on medium coals for about an hour or until a knife stuck into the center comes out clean.

Place the pot on your grill to avoid burning the bottom of the bread and pop a few coals on top to aid in browning.

 Tips

You can get your gourmet on and add a variety of toppings to your beer bread like roasted sunflower seeds, chopped onion, sesame seeds or (you guessed it!) cheese.

Wheat Heart Campfire Bread

What You Need

- 3 1/2 Cups bread flour
- 1 Sachet instant yeast
- 1 tsp. Salt
- 6 tsp. Maple syrup
- 1/4 Cup (60 ml) cooking oil
- 1–2 Cups of lukewarm water

Instructions

Save a couple of teaspoons of flour for kneading. Mix the rest of the flour, yeast and salt. Make a well in the center of your dry ingredients and slowly add the syrup and oil, stirring as you go. Now add just enough water to make a dough that binds nicely, but isn't sticky. Dust hands with the flour you set aside. Knead the dough until it is elastic and smooth. Leave it to rise in a warm spot. When it has doubled in volume (usually about 30 minutes), knead it again for ten minutes. Place the dough in your well-oiled camping pot and leave it to rise again for 15-20 minutes. Now put the pot on the coals and use your tongs to place a couple of coals on the top of the pot. Bake until a knife stuck into the center comes out clean.

Tips

You can substitute 6 teaspoons of sugar for the maple syrup.

Place the pot on your grill to avoid burning the bottom of the bread.

Roll small balls of this dough and pop on top of chili or stew to make dumplings.

Roll small balls of dough, flatten with your palm and, using tongs, place directly onto coals to make tandoori bread. When the edges brown, turn the bread over and bake on the other side.

Caramelized Onions *on the grill*

What You Need

- 1 Large onion
- 2 tbsp. Butter
- 1 Beef boullion cube
- Salt and pepper to taste
- Foil

Instructions

Place the onion onto the center of a double-folded piece of foil. Cut it into eight equal segments, taking care to only cut 3/4 of the way through the onion. Break up the beef bullion cube and sprinkle over the top. Season to taste and dot with butter.

Fold the edges of the foil up and scrunch it together at the top, leaving a small hole to let the steam out. Grill for 25 minutes or until tender.

 Tips

If you are making this meal later in your expedition, you can substitute the butter with olive oil.

For a vegetarian option, use a vegetable stock cube or garlic salt.

Catch of the Day

What You Need

- 1 Large whole fish
- 1 Medium onion (diced)
- 1 Tomato (diced)

- 1 tbsp. Olive oil
- Salt and pepper to taste
- Foil

Instructions

Lay the fish on its side in the center of a piece of foil. Stuff the cavity with onion, tomato and olive oil. Season to taste. Fold the edges of the foil over the fish. Wrap the whole fish again in another sheet of foil. Grill directly on the coals for 20 minutes on both sides.

Serves 4-6

 # Tips

Try this meal with lemon and dill instead of onion and tomato.

Add chilies for a spicier recipe.

Chicken Foil Folders

What You Need

- 1 lb. (500g) Skinless, bone-less chicken breast (cubed)
- 2 Onions (diced)
- 1 Red bell pepper (seeded and cut into strips)
- 2 Cloves of garlic (crushed)
- 4 Small potatoes (diced)
- 1/4 Cup olive oil
- Juice from one lemon
- Foil

Instructions

Toss ingredients together in a bowl & divide into 4 portions. Place each portion on a piece of foil. Fold the sides of the foil up and seal the edges. Cover with another piece of foil. Grill for 40 minutes or until potatoes are tender.

Serves 4-6

 # Tips

If you are making this meal later in your expedition, you can substitute the chicken with fresh-caught fish or with chorizo or kielbasa sausage.

For a vegetarian option, omit the chicken and add zucchini.

Chicken on a Beer Can

What You Need

- 1 Medium chicken
- 1 Can of beer
- 1 Bunch of fresh rosemary (chopped)
- 2 tsp. Olive oil
- 1 tsp. Dried thyme
- 1/2 tsp. Red pepper flakes
- Juice of 1 lemon
- Salt and pepper to taste

Instructions

Combine the rosemary, olive oil, thyme, pepper flakes and lemon juice in a bowl. Rub the outside of the chicken with the marinade and stuff the remaining marinade into the chicken cavity. Open the beer and drink half of it. Push the top of the beer can into the cavity (don't spill the beer). Now place the beer can (with the chicken on it) onto the grill over the fire. Place a large pot over the chicken and barbecue until done (1 to 1.5 hours). Season with salt and pepper.

Serves 4-6

 ## Tips

Be sure to pack a pot that is big enough to fit over the chicken. If you don't have space in your pack, make a foil tent to place over the chicken instead.

If you are making this chicken after day two, ensure that the chicken is frozen and well wrapped before you leave.

Potato Pockets

What You Need

- 5 Medium potatoes (washed and thinly sliced)
- 1 Medium onion sliced
- 1/3 Chicken bouillon cube in 1/3 cup hot water

- 6 tbsp. Butter or olive oil
- 1/3 Cup cheddar cheese (thinly sliced)
- Foil

Instructions

Lay out a sheet of foil that is about 20"X20" (50 cmX50 cm).
Spread a layer of potatoes in the middle, leaving a 4" (10cm)
border around the edges. Alternate with a layer of sliced onion
until you have used all the potato and onion. Dot with butter or
pour over olive oil. If you are using cheese, sprinkle it over the top.
Season with salt and pepper. Fold the sides of the foil up and seal
the corners so you are making a bowl. Pour over the chicken broth
and cook over a hot fire. Tent a piece of foil over the top and grill
for 30 minutes or until potatoes are tender.

Serves 4-6

 Tips

If you are making this meal in the first two days of your expedition,
use butter and add the cheese. For use later in the trip, use olive
oil instead of butter and omit the cheese.

Fried Bass
with Salt and Vinegar Chips, Mate!

What You Need

- 1/4 Cup oil
- 3 Eggs
- 1 tbsp. Water
- 4 Bass fillets (skinned)

- 1/2 Cup flour
- 1 Small pack salt and vinegar crisps
- 1 Lemon (cut into wedges)

Instructions

Mix eggs and water together in a bowl with a fork. Crush the salt and vinegar chips and place them in a plate. Place the flour in another plate. Put the oil in a pan over the fire and heat gently. Lay each fillet in the flour (do both sides) and then in the egg mixture and finally in the chips. Fry for about 4 minutes on each side or until lightly browned. Serve with lemon wedges. Better than a Bass-o-matic!

Serves 4-6

 ## Tips

See page 134 for notes on how to catch and fillet a bass.

You can leave out the chips for a simple recipe and add salt and pepper to taste.

Good Ol' Stew

What You Need

- 1/4 Cup vegetable oil
- 2lbs (1 kg) Stewing beef cut into cubes
- 1 Medium onion (chopped)
- 2 Cups cloves garlic (minced)
- 4 Cups water
- 1 Beef stock cube
- 1 Can chopped tomatoes
- 4 Bay leaves
- 1 tsp. Salt
- 1/4 tsp. Pepper
- 1 Carrot (sliced)
- 4 Potatoes (diced)

Instructions

Place the oil in a large pot on the fire. Fry beef until browned. Add onion and garlic and fry until translucent. Crumble the stock cube into the pot and add water. Add tomatoes, bay leaves, salt, pepper, carrot and potatoes and put the lid on. Simmer for 20-30 minutes until the stew has reduced and looks thick and yummy - just the way you like it.

Serves 4

 # Tips

If you are making this after day one, freeze the beef before you leave so it will last longer.

Substitute lentils or dehydrated soya mince if your trip will last longer than a few days and for a vegetarian option.

Atomic Boogaloo Chili

What You Need

- 2 lbs (1kg) Ground beef
- 2 Medium yellow onions, chopped
- 2 Garlic cloves, minced
- 2 tbsp. Oil
- 3 Tomatoes, chopped
- 1 Can tomato paste
- 1 Diced green chili

- 1 tsp. Cayenne (or to taste)
- 1 tsp. Salt
- 1 tsp. Ground cumin
- 1 tsp. Oregano
- 2 Bouillon beef cubes dissolved in 2 cups warm water
- 1 Cup water
- 1 15 oz Can red kidney beans

Instructions

Brown onions, beef and garlic in the oil. Add tomatoes, tomato paste, chili, cayenne, salt, cumin and oregano. Cook for 2 minutes until flavors have mixed. Add bouillon, water and beans and simmer for 30 minutes.

Serves 4-6

 # Tips

If tomatoes will get squashed in your bag, opt for a can of whole tomatoes instead.

Make this chili at home and take it with you if you don't want to spend time cooking.

Freeze ground beef and wrap in newspaper or keep in a cooler if you aren't cooking chili on day one of your trip. Substitute elk or deer (or a mixture) for ground beef.

Reduce weight by substituting dry beans for canned beans. Soak the beans for 8 hours overnight. Rinse and boil for 10 minutes to neutralize a toxin contained in their skin, then simmer for 45-60 minutes until they are creamy inside. Don't add salt as this hardens the skin.

The longer you cook chili, the better it tastes. If you have a fire on the go, scrape some coals to the side and leave your chili to simmer until you are ready to eat.

For a vegetarian option, use dehydrated soya mince instead of ground beef and vegetable stock instead of boullion.

Shepherd's Pie in a Pot

What You Need

- 1 Medium onion (chopped)
- 2 tbsp. Olive oil
- 1/2 lb. (200g) Ground beef
- 1 Beef bouillon cube
- 2 Large potatoes (peeled and chopped)

- 2 tbsp. Butter
- Salt and Pepper to taste
- 1 Cup grated cheese (optional)

Instructions

In a small pot, boil potatoes until tender. Then add butter, salt and pepper to taste and mash. Set aside.

In a small skillet, heat the olive oil and add onions. Fry until translucent. Add the ground beef and cook until browned. Break the bouillon cube into the ground beef and add a little water. Cook for another 10 minutes until liquid is reduced by half.

Remove skillet from the fire, top the ground beef mixture with the mashed potatoes and sprinkle the cheese on top. Return to the fire until cheese is melted.

Serves 4

 Tips

Chilies or hot sauce will add a little spice to your life here.

If you are making this dish later in the trip, or for a vegetarian option, use dehydrated soya mince and omit the cheese and butter.

Veggie Kebabs

What You Need

- 1/2 Pineapple
- 1 Red pepper
- 1 Zucchini
- 1 Cup halloumi cheese (cubed)
- 3 tbsp. Honey
- 1/4 Cup olive oil
- 2 Lemons
- 1 Chopped chili
- Skewers
- Large sealable plastic bag or container

Instructions

Soak the kebab skewers in water so that they don't burn.

Juice the lemons into the bag or bowl. Add the honey, salt and olive oil to the lemon juice. Add chili to taste.

Chop the pineapple, red pepper, and zucchini into medium-sized cubes and place in the lemon marinade. Leave to get all covered in lemony goodness for about 30 minutes.

Thread the veggie chunks and cheese onto skewers and roast over the flames. Baste by pouring the remaining marinade over the kebabs.

Serves 4

 # Tips

For days 2-4, freeze the cheese before you leave and keep wrapped in newspaper and a foil bag. Keep your pack in a shady, cool place.

To make these later in the trip, omit the cheese and use a red onion instead.

Sticky Pork Chops

What You Need

- 6 Pork chops
- 1/2 Cup balsamic vinegar
- 1/2 Cup olive oil
- 2 tsp. Chopped rosemary
- 3 tsp. Honey
- 3 tsp. Soya sauce
- 2 tsp. Chutney

Instructions

Combine marinade ingredients in a sealable plastic bag. Pop your chops in and leave for a couple of hours so that they can soak up that juicy goodness! Place chops on the grill and cook over hot coals. Leave the marinade in the bag and drizzle it over the meat while it cooks.

Serves 4

 ## Tips

Use dried rosemary if you don't have fresh herbs.

Substitute apricot jam for the chutney.

You can mix the marinade before you leave and simply keep it in the sealable plastic bag.

If you are using this recipe after day one, freeze the chops in the marinade so that they will last longer.

Marinated Flank Steak

What You Need

- 2 lbs. (1 kg) Flank steak
- 1/2 Cup soya sauce
- 1 Clove garlic (minced)
- 2 tbsp. Brown sugar

- 1 tsp. Ginger (minced)
- 2 tbsp. Lemon juice
- 2 tbsp. Oil
- Pepper to taste

Instructions

Combine ingredients in a sealable plastic bag and leave for a couple of hours. Place steak on the grill and cook over hot coals. Leave the marinade in the bag and drizzle it over the meat while it cooks. This is, without a doubt, the bomb diggity.

Serves 4

 # Tips

If you are making this on day 2-3 of your trip, place the flank steak & marinade in a sealable plastic bag and freeze. Keep in a small cooler or wrap in newspaper and keep in the shade to maintain freshness.

Can't find flank steak? No problem! You can use any kind of steak you want. You can even use venison, chicken, ostrich or crocodile - this marinade works on just about anything!

Just Desserts

Dessert Stomach, We Salute You!

Ah, thank your lucky stars for the dessert stomach; that noble organ that allows you to find space for dessert no matter how much you ate for dinner.

Tips for Happy Camping

 Burn sage in your campfire to keep the mosquitoes at bay. You can buy wild sage in dried bunches which you put a flame to and then set aside so it can smolder.

 Learn to recognize poison ivy, poison oak and wild parsnip to avoid getting painful burns or rashes. Always carry baking soda with you. If you get an itchy rash, make a paste with baking soda and water and apply to the affected area. Works great for bug bites too!

 Drinking a teaspoon of baking soda in a little water will still even the most raging heartburn.

What's on the Menu?

Banana Boat 120

Campfire Fondue 122

S'mores in a Cone 124

Peach Cobbler 126

Roast Apple on a Stick 128

Banana Boat

What You Need

- 4 Ripe Bananas
- 4 tsp. Chocolate chips
- 4 tbsp. Marshmallows
- Foil

Instructions

Place a banana on the foil. Slice the banana along the inside curve, leaving about an inch on both ends uncut. Pull open the peel and spoon in the marshmallows and top with some chocolate chips.

Fold the sides of the foil up around the banana so it can stay upright; leave the top part exposed so the marshmallows can brown. Cook for 10 minutes on the coals.

Serves 4

 Tips

If you are making this after the first day of your trip, take green bananas so that they can stay fresh for longer.

Take care when packing so that your bananas don't get squished.

Campfire Fondue

What You Need

- Marshmallows
- Strawberries

- Milk chocolate

Instructions

Over medium coals, melt the chocolate in a pot. Put marshmallows and strawberries on sticks and dip them into the chocolate.

 ## Tips

Dip fruit, cookies, wafers and nuts and anything else that grabs your fancy.

Use your utensils or small sticks to dip your goodies into the hot chocolate to avoid burns.

Always volunteer to do the dishes on Campfire Fondue nights so that you get to lick out that chocolate pot!

S'mores in a Cone

What You Need

- 6 Ice cream cones
- 1/2 Cup chocolate chips
- 1/2 Cup mini marshmallows
- Foil

Instructions

Take the ice cream cones and sprinkle a layer of chocolate chips in the bottom. Cover with a layer of mini marshmallows. Continue to layer chocolate chips and marshmallows until the cone is full. Now wrap in foil and cook over the coals for 3-5 minutes or until the marshmallows are melted.

Serves 4-6

 ## Tips

Be careful when packing the wafer cones to ensure that they aren't crushed by the time you are ready for this tasty treat. Use a plastic container or pop them in your shoes and then in your backpack. But do yourself (and everyone else) a favor and put them in a plastic bag first because, you know... feet.

Peach Cobbler

What You Need

- 4 Peaches halved and pitted
- 4 tbsp. Brown sugar
- 4 tsp. Butter

- 4 tbsp. Oats
- Foil

Instructions

Place the peach halves on the foil and top with butter and oats. Sprinkle brown sugar on the top. Wrap and place on the hot coals for 10-15 minutes until peaches are cooked through.

Serves 4

 # Tips

For a more decadent dessert, add chocolate chips, nuts or substitute granola for the oats.

Want to blow the minds of your fellow campers? Use the pie crust recipe from the BBQ Pie page 78. Roll out the dough. Divide the dough into 8 parts, line 4 greased metal cups with dough, spoon in the peach cobbler filling and top with the remaining 4 pieces of dough. Bake on the fire for individual peach pie desserts. YES!

Roast Apple

on a Stick

What You Need

- 4 Small apples
- Brown sugar
- Cinnamon

Instructions

Push a stick through the middle of each apple. Hold over the fire, turning regularly. As the apple bakes, the skin will brown and the juice will drip out. Remove from fire and leave to cool for a couple of minutes.

Peel the skin off, but leave the stick in. Roll in cinnamon sugar and eat on the stick.

Serves 4

 # Tips

Sprinkle trail mix or granola over the apples for a crunchy crust.

You can use peaches for this recipe too.

On the Side

Counter Intelligence

Learning to cook is the best form of 'counter intelligence' for those who like to live an independent life off the beaten track. Cooking is easy and almost as much fun as eating. Here are a few of the basics that will turn your campfire dinner from pitiful to profound. Happy camping!

Tips for Happy Camping

 Make your own natural tick repellent. Mix one part tea tree oil with two parts water in a spray bottle. Spray on pants, socks and shoes. Always check for ticks after hiking or walking in the wild, especially in long grass.

 Get some fresh greens on the run with easy DIY sprouts. Punch a couple of holes in the lid of a Mason jar. Add 1/3 cup lentils and 2 cups water. Leave for 24 hours and drain water. Rinse lentils twice a day and drain. In 48 hours, you will have super fresh sprouts!

 Substitute your tent pegs for solar lights to shed some light on your campsite and prevent other campers from tripping over guide ropes.

What's on the Menu?

DIY Spices   132
Drinks   133
How to Fillet a Fish   134
Suggested Menus   136

Homemade Taco Seasoning

- 1 tbsp. Chili powder
- 1 tsp. Smoked paprika
- 1/2 tsp. Ground coriander
- 1/2 tbsp. Ground cumin
- 1 tsp. Cornstarch
- 1 tsp. Kosher salt
- 1/4 tsp. Cayenne pepper

Put all ingredients into a jar and shake it up. Use 2 tablespoons for 1 pound (450g) of meat.

Basic Curry Spice

- 2 tsp. Ground coriander
- 1 tsp. Ground cumin
- 1/4 tsp. Turmeric
- 1/4 tsp. Cayenne or chili powder

Mix together and keep in a sealed container.

Chai Tea

- 1 1/2 Cups water
- 1/2 Cup milk
- Sugar to taste
- 1/4 tsp. Cardamom

- 1 Cinnamon stick
- 4 Black tea bags
- 1/2 Inch fresh
  ginger, finely chopped

Heat water, cardamom, cinnamon and ginger to boiling then remove pot from fire. Add teabags and steep for 5 minutes. Discard teabags. Add milk and sugar and return to the fire. Simmer gently for 10 minutes. Makes 2 cups.

Ginger Tea

- 3 Inch nub of ginger

- Honey to taste

Slice the ginger into a pot of clean water. Leave to boil for about 15 minutes. Pour into cups and sweeten with honey. Makes 2 cups.

Gluehwein

- 3/4 Cup water
- 3/4 Cup white sugar
- 1 Cinnamon stick

- 1 Orange
- 10 Whole cloves
- 1 Bottle red wine

In a pot, combine water, sugar and cinnamon stick and bring to a simmer. Cut the orange & squeeze juice into the pot. Peel off sections of the orange peel and press the cloves in. Pop the peels into the pot. When the syrup thickens, remove peels and add the wine. Heat to warm, but not simmering. Serve immediately. Add a vanilla pod, grated nutmeg and star anise if you want more flavor.

How to: *Fillet a Fish*

What You Need

- Fillet knife (make sure that this is super sharp)
- Cutting board

- Fish
- Bowl of cold water

How to Fillet a Fish

Yay you caught a fish! Well done Indiana Jones, now you can really impress your camp buddies by cleaning it and serving it for dinner. It's easy, just take your time and work carefully and you will master this great life skill in no time.

Remove the scales first. Hold the fish by the tail and, with the back of your knife, scrape from the tail to the head. The scales should fly off. Lay the fish flat on the cutting board with its spine facing you. Locate the pectoral fin just above the gills. Hold the knife at a 45 degree angle, next to the pectoral fin, with the bottom tilted to the fish head. Make a single cut down across the width of the fish from spine to belly. Cut down to the spine, but not through it. Now angle the knife the other way and slice down the length of the fish from gill to tail so you have one solid fillet. Repeat on the other side for your second fillet. Rinse the fillets in cold water.

How to Clean a Fish

If you want to cook the whole fish, it's easier to clean. Remove the scales first. Hold the fish by the tail and, with the back of your knife, scrape from the tail to the head. The scales should fly off. Cut off the pectoral fins using two 45 degree angle cuts on both sides of the fin. Lay the fish on its side with the belly facing you. Lay one hand on the top of the fish and then cut through the middle of the belly from the gills to the tail. Reach in and remove the innards. Wash the whole fish and cavity with cold water. Your fish is ready to cook!

Note: Be responsible when discarding scales and innards. Dig a hole to bury them and ensure that you don't create a mess in the campsite for the next campers to deal with. Wildlife may also be attracted to the smell of fresh fish, so discard bits you don't want away from your campsite.

Suggested Menus

Because We Care...

Not good at putting menus together? We've got you covered! These ready-made menus will help you to plan your trip and do the shopping too. These menus are designed for four people, so adjust as necessary to suit the number in your own posse.

Menus one and two use perishables so use these on the first two to three days of your trip. Number three and four are for use in the latter half of longer camping trips.

You should be snacking on fruits and having sides of veggies and salads.

Menu One

Breakfast: Badass Breakfast Burrito
(add some of the salsa you will use on your nachos)
Lunch: Toastie Wraps
Snack: Nature's Nachos
(add the other half of the avocado you used for breakfast)
Dinner: Fried Bass with Vinegar Chips with Tomato Peach Salad

Shopping List

- 7 eggs
- 1/4 cup and 4 tbsp. oil
- 1 avocado
- 2 onions
- 1 chorizo sausage
- salt and pepper
- 4 burritos
- 12 tortillas
- 1 can of salsa
- 1 tbsp. water
- 4 bass fillets

- 1/2 cup flour
- 1 small packed salt and vinegar crisps
- 1 lemon
- 3 cups grated cheese
- 6 tomatoes
- 4 peaches
  (or can of peach slices)
- 1 red onion
- 2 tbsp. apple cider vinegar

Menu Two

Breakfast: Good Old Fry Up
Lunch: Toasted Ham and Cheese Sandwich
Snack: Potato Skins
Dinner: Shepherd's Pie in a Pot with Beet and Feta Salad

Shopping List

- 1/2 cup oil
- 1 loaf bread
- 3 eggs
- 2 tbsp. water
- 8 slices of ham
- 6 tbsp. mayonnaise
- 2 cups grated cheese
- salt to taste
- 1 medium onion
- 1/2 lb. ground beef
- 1 beef bouillon cube

- 2 large potatoes
- 2 tbsp. butter
- avocado
- 1 tsp. lime juice or apple cider vinegar
- hot sauce
- 4 beets
- 2 tbsp. white vinegar
- 1/4 red onion
- feta cheese

Menu Three

Breakfast: Toad in the Hole
(add fruit on the side for a healthy vitamin boost)
Lunch: Tacos
Snack: Nature's Nachos
Dinner: Sticky Pork Chops and Asparagus and Balsamic Vinegar

Shopping List

- 6 tortillas
- 1 can of salsa
- 2 cups grated Cheese
- 6 tbsp. oil
- 1 lb. ground beef
- 2 tomatoes
- 1 onion
- 1 avocado
- Foil
- 6 pork chops
- 1/2 cup & 2 tbsp. balsamic

- 1/2 cup olive oil
- 2 tsp. chopped rosemary
- 3 tsp. honey
- 3 tsp. soya sauce
- 2 tsp. chutney
- 4 rashers of bacon
- 4 slices of bread
- 4 eggs
- 1 bunch asparagus spears
- 4 tbsp. water
- Salt and pepper to taste

You can get a pack of taco spice or make your own using:

- 1 tbsp. chili powder
- 1 tsp. smoked paprika
- 1/2 tsp. ground coriander
- 1/2 tablespoon ground cumin

- 1 tsp. cornstarch
- 1 tsp. kosher salt
- 1/4 tsp. cayenne pepper

Menu Four

Breakfast: Pancakes
(add fruit on the side for a healthy vitamin boost)
Lunch: Baked Avocado
Snack: Popcorn Pockets
Dinner: Grateful Red Chili
Dessert: Roast Apples

Shopping List

- 2 tbsp. popcorn kernels
- 6 tbsp. oil
- foil
- string
- 4 1/2 cups flour
- 40 ml (1.3 oz) baking powder
- 7 tsp. salt
- 1 1/2 cups shortening
- 1 1/2 cups non-fat powdered milk
- 1/2 egg
- 1/2 cup water
- 2 avocados
- pepper
- chili flakes
- 4 medium tomato

- 3 medium onion
- feta cheese (optional)
- foil
- 2 lbs ground beef (or use dehydrated soya mince)
- 2 garlic cloves
- 1 can tomato paste
- 1 diced green chili
- 1 tsp. cayenne (or to taste)
- 1 tsp. ground cumin
- 1 tsp. oregano
- 2 bouillon beef cubes
- 1 (15 ounce) can red kidney beans (use dry if too heavy)
- 4 small apples
- brown sugar and cinnamon

Scary Stuff

Get Your Spook On!

No camping trip is complete without the requisite campfire story that sets your knees aquiver. Here are some super scary stories that will keep you from wandering off... you have been warned!

SSSSamantha

Send an accomplice into the woods near your campsite

It was a dark and stormy night at camp Buttercup and the girls had been caught in the rain out in the woods. As they struggled through the slippery mud and fading light, they were only too happy to see the twinkling lights of their bungalows.

The other councilors started on dinner while the camp leader, Deidre took a quick roll call.

"Damn!" she said, "Samantha is missing. The rest of you stay here and take care of the girls, I'll go find her," she instructed the councilors. Armed with a flashlight and raincoat, she headed out into the night.

Suddenly there was a loud crash as lightning struck the ground near the camp and the lights went out. The wind howled and slammed the doors and the girls screamed and huddled together.

In the distance, they could hear Deidre shouting for Samantha. "Ssssssssssssssamantha!" she shouted and her flashlight zig zagged through the trees and her voice grew fainter and fainter until they could hear her no more.

Tired and exhausted, the girls fell asleep right after dinner. In the middle of the night they were wakened by a loud crash as the door flew open and the flashlight and raincoat fell into the middle of the floor. The girls screamed and the councilors ran outside, but there was no sign of anyone.

Samantha and Deidre were never seen again, but some say that if you walk these woods at night, you can still hear Deirdre calling "Ssssssssamantha."
Shhh... can you hear that?

Get your accomplice to shout "Sssssmantha!!" really loudly from the woods.

The Good Sister

My sister Sarah has been sent away again. I hate it when she goes away. And every time she comes back she stays for shorter periods of time. The doctors always say she is perfectly fine, but mom and dad say that she is just very clever and an expert manipulator.

Still they feel guilty and so they always take her back. Especially since I cry and beg them to let her stay with us for a while. Of course, when she returns, they tell her this is the last time. That if it happens again they won't let her out. That they will lock her up forever.

She cries and promises that she will be a good girl.

But it never lasts. Before long, the neighborhood cats start going missing and they turn up in her toy trunk. Their blood smeared on their owners walls in a kind of gruesome graffiti.

And mom and dad get very, very scared.

And then she goes back & they lock her up again.

I hate it when she goes away because I'm lonely and I miss her. I have no one to play with.

But most of all, I hate it when she goes away, because then I have to pretend to be good until she returns.

Clown Around

After a sleepover at a friend's house, the kids started saying that they were scared of the clown that lived in their room. Of course we don't have any clowns in the house as my wife finds them creepy. At first we thought that they were just making things up, but after the second day, we started getting annoyed.

You see, the friend that they had a sleepover with isn't always the best influence and we became convinced that they had watched a scary movie while they were there. On the third night they refused to sleep in their own beds and cried until we let them sleep in ours.

On the fourth night, we insisted they return to their rooms, but they were terrified and took hours to get to sleep while we were made to look behind doors, under beds and in closets to prove that there was no clown to be found.
Still, they woke up screaming in the night and there

was no sleep for anyone.

And now it's Saturday afternoon and the kids and my wife, exhausted from their nightmares, are napping. And there he is; leaning his forehead against the window. His eyes are yellow and bloodshot and the white makeup on his face is cracked and flaking.

His red mouth is more of a gash than a smile and a single black tear is painted on his cheek. We stare at each other for a while before he turns and walks into the house while I'm out here, watering the garden.

Thank You's

I am profoundly grateful to David whose drive and continued support make all that is wonderful and beautiful possible.

Thanks also to the creative genius of Eddie Ruminski and Cornelius Quiring who have made something really special.

Thanks to Ian for the photos and Chris 'Eagle eye' Heffler for keeping us on the straight and narrow.

---

theflamingmarshmallow.com

Simple, delicious campfire recipes designed for times when epic badassery is afoot. Come adventurer, sit a while by the fire with us and let's share a meal, a story and a laugh.

Twitter @greenmoxie
Instagram @greenmoxie

I'm not a chef. I am a traveler, adventurer and world-renowned horseradish whisperer. I grew up in Durban, South Africa, where there are no seasons, just one glorious summer so naturally, we cook outside.

I spent a decade of my life traveling, enjoying the wonder that is international cuisine, perpetually drawn to food cooked on fires. From the tandoori ovens of India to the street woks of Thailand and the kebab barbecues of the Middle East, I collected these recipes & tips that I've been so honored to share here with you.

Lightning Source UK Ltd.
Milton Keynes UK
UKHW021813211218
334317UK00006B/154/P